THE UNITED NATIONS was established, in the aftermath of a devastating war, to help stabilize international relations and give peace a more secure foundation.

Amid the threat of nuclear war and seemingly endless regional conflicts, peacekeeping has become an overriding concern of the United Nations, and the activities of the blue-helmeted peacekeepers have emerged as among the most visible.

But the United Nations is much more than a peacekeeper and forum for conflict resolution. Often without attracting attention, the United Nations and its family of agencies are engaged in a vast array of work that seeks to improve people's lives around the world.

Child survival and development. Environmental protection. Human rights. Health and medical research. Alleviation of poverty and economic development. Agricultural development and fisheries. Education. The advancement of women. Emergency and disaster relief. Air and sea travel. Peaceful uses of atomic energy. Labour and workers' rights. The list goes on.

Here, in brief, is a sampling of what the United Nations and its component bodies have accomplished since 1945, when the world organization was founded.

1 PROMOTING DEVELOPMENT

The United Nations has devoted its attention and resources to promoting living standards and human skills and potential throughout the world. Since 2000, this work has been guided by the Millennium Development Goals (MDGs). The UN system's annual expenditures for development, excluding the international financial institutions, amount to more than $10 billion. For instance, the UN Development Programme, with staff in 166 countries, leads the UN's work on eradicating extreme poverty and promoting good governance in the developing world. UNICEF works in 157 countries and spends more than $1.2 billion a year, primarily on child protection, immunization, fighting HIV/AIDS and girls' education. UNCTAD helps countries make the most of their trade opportunities for development purposes. In addition, the World Bank provides developing countries with loans and grants totalling around $18 billion-$20 billion a year and has supported more than 9,500 development projects since 1947. Virtually all funds for development aid come from contributions donated by countries.

2 PROMOTING DEMOCRACY

The UN has helped to promote and strengthen democratic institutions and practices around the world. It has enabled people in many countries to participate in free and fair elections, including in Cambodia, Namibia, El Salvador, Eritrea, Mozambique, Nicaragua, South Africa, Kosovo and East Timor. It has provided electoral advice and assistance, including the monitoring of results, to more than 90 countries, often at decisive moments in their history, as in Afghanistan, Iraq and Burundi.

3 PROMOTING HUMAN RIGHTS

Since the General Assembly adopted the Universal Declaration of Human Rights in 1948, the United Nations has helped to enact dozens of comprehensive agreements on political, civil, economic, social and cultural rights. By investigating individual complaints, the UN human rights bodies have focused world attention on cases of torture, disappearance and arbitrary detention and have generated international pressure to be brought to bear on Governments to improve their human rights records.

4 MAINTAINING PEACE AND SECURITY

By sending a total of 60 peacekeeping and observer missions to the world's trouble spots, as of 2005, the United Nations has been able to restore calm sufficiently to allow the negotiating process to go forward, saving millions of people from becoming casualties of war. There are at present 16 peacekeeping operations around the world.

5 MAKING PEACE

Since 1945, the UN has assisted in negotiating more than 170 peace settlements that have ended regional conflicts. Examples include ending the Iran-Iraq war, facilitating the withdrawal of Soviet troops from Afghanistan and ending the civil wars in El Salvador and Guatemala. The United Nations has used quiet diplomacy to avert imminent wars.

6 PROTECTING THE ENVIRONMENT

The United Nations is working to solve global environmental problems. As an international forum for building consensus and negotiating agreements, the UN is tackling global problems like climate change, ozone layer depletion, toxic waste, loss of forests and species, and air and water pollution. Unless these problems are addressed, markets and economies will not be sustainable in the long term, as environmental losses are depleting the natural "capital" on which growth and human survival are based.

7 PREVENTING NUCLEAR PROLIFERATION

The United Nations, through the International Atomic Energy Agency (IAEA), helps to ensure that countries using nuclear technologies are not secretly developing nuclear weapons. Hundreds of nuclear facilities are safeguarded by IAEA in more than 70 countries. To date, there are 237 safeguards agreements in force with 152 States.

8 PROMOTING SELF-DETERMINATION AND INDEPENDENCE

When the UN was established in 1945, 750 million people — almost a third of the world population — lived in Non-Self-governing Territories dependent on colonial Powers. The United Nations played a role in bringing about independence in more than 80 countries that are now sovereign nations.

9 PROSECUTING WAR CRIMINALS

UN tribunals established for the former Yugoslavia and for Rwanda have convicted war criminals and put them behind bars, have developed important case law on genocide and human rights and have provided a measure of justice that has been taken very seriously by the people of the affected regions.

10 ENDING APARTHEID IN SOUTH AFRICA

By imposing measures ranging from an arms embargo to a convention against segregated sporting events, the United Nations was a major factor in bringing about the downfall of the apartheid system. In 1994, elections in which all South Africans were allowed to participate on an equal basis led to the establishment of a multiracial Government.

"WE STAND HERE TODAY TO SALUTE THE UNITED NATIONS ORGANIZATION AND ITS MEMBER STATES, BOTH SINGLY AND COLLECTIVELY, FOR JOINING FORCES WITH THE MASSES OF OUR PEOPLE IN A COMMON STRUGGLE THAT HAS BROUGHT ABOUT OUR EMANCIPATION AND PUSHED BACK THE FRONTIERS OF RACISM."

— PRESIDENT NELSON MANDELA in his address to the UN General Assembly in 1994, the year in which the first free multiracial elections were held in South Africa.

11 STRENGTHENING INTERNATIONAL LAW

Over 500 multilateral treaties — on human rights, terrorism, international crime, refugees, disarmament, commodities and the oceans — have been enacted through the efforts of the United Nations.

12 PROVIDING HUMANITARIAN AID TO REFUGEES

More than 50 million refugees fleeing war, famine or persecution have received aid from the UN High Commissioner for Refugees since 1951, in a continuing effort that often involves other agencies. The organization seeks long-term or "durable" solutions by helping refugees repatriate to their homeland if conditions warrant, or by helping them to integrate in their countries of asylum or to resettle in third countries. There are more than 19 million refugees, asylum-seekers and internally displaced persons, mostly women and children, who are receiving food, shelter, medical aid, education and repatriation assistance from the UN.

13 ALLEVIATING RURAL POVERTY IN DEVELOPING COUNTRIES

The International Fund for Agricultural Development (IFAD) has developed a system for providing credit, often in very small amounts, that enables rural poor people to overcome poverty. Since starting operations in 1978, IFAD has invested more than $8.5 billion in 676 projects and programmes, benefiting more than 250 million people. All IFAD funds come from voluntary contributions from countries.

14 AIDING PALESTINE REFUGEES

As the global community strives for a lasting peace between Israelis and Palestinians, the UN Relief and Works Agency for Palestine refugees in the Near East (UNRWA), a relief and human development agency, has assisted four generations of Palestinian refugees with education, health care, social services, microfinance and emergency aid. Today, over 4 million refugees in the Middle East are registered with UNRWA.

15 FOCUSING ON AFRICAN DEVELOPMENT

Africa continues to be a high priority for the United Nations. In 1986, the UN convened a special session to drum up international support for African economic recovery and development. In 2001, African Heads of State adopted the continent's own plan, the New Partnership for Africa's Development, which was endorsed by the General Assembly in 2002 as the main framework for channelling international support to Africa. The continent receives 33 per cent of UN system expenditures for development, the largest share among regions. All UN agencies have special programmes to benefit Africa.

16 PROMOTING WOMEN'S WELL-BEING

The United Nations has helped to promote women's equality and well-being. The UN Development Fund for Women (UNIFEM) and the International Research and Training Institute for the Advancement of Women (INSTRAW) have helped to improve women's quality of life and promote women's rights in over 100 countries. INSTRAW carries out research and training activities and UNIFEM supports projects that seek to eliminate violence against women, reverse the spread of HIV/AIDS and promote women's economic security — for instance, by increasing their access to work and their rights to land and inheritance. All UN agencies must take into account the needs of women.

17 PROMOTING WOMEN'S RIGHTS

A long-term objective of the United Nations has been to improve the lives of women and to empower women to have greater control over their lives. The UN organized the first-ever World Women's Conference (Mexico City, 1975), which together with other conferences during the UN-sponsored International Women's Decade set the agenda for advancing women's rights. The 1979 UN Convention on the Elimination of All Forms of Discrimination against Women, ratified by 180 countries, has helped to promote the rights of women worldwide.

18 PROVIDING SAFE DRINKING WATER

During the first UN decade on water (1981-1990), more than a billion people gained access to safe drinking water for the first time in their lives. An additional 1.1 billion people gained access to safe drinking water between 1990 and 2002. In 2003, the International Year of Freshwater raised awareness of the importance of protecting this precious resource. The second international water decade (2005-2015) aims to reduce by half the proportion of people without access to safe drinking water.

19 WIPING OUT POLIO

Poliomyelitis has been eliminated from all but six countries — Afghanistan, Egypt, India, Niger, Nigeria and Pakistan — as a result of the Global Polio Eradication Initiative, the largest international public health effort to date. Thanks to the Initiative, spearheaded by the World Health Organization, UNICEF, Rotary International and the U.S. Centers for Disease Control and Prevention, nearly 5 million children are walking who would otherwise have been paralysed by polio. A disease which once crippled children in 125 countries around the world is on the verge of being eradicated.

20 RESPONDING TO HIV/AIDS

The Joint United Nations Programme on HIV/AIDS (UNAIDS) coordinates global action against an epidemic that is affecting nearly 40 million people. It works in more than 130 countries to provide universal access to HIV prevention and treatment services, as well as reduce the vulnerability of individuals and communities and alleviate the impact of the epidemic. UNAIDS brings together the expertise of its 10 co-sponsoring UN organizations.

21 ERADICATING SMALLPOX

A 13-year effort by the World Health Organization resulted in the complete eradication of smallpox from the planet in 1980. The eradication has saved an estimated $1 billion a year in vaccination and monitoring, almost three times the cost of eliminating the scourge itself.

22 FIGHTING PARASITIC DISEASES

A World Health Organization programme in 11 West African countries has virtually wiped out river blindness (onchocerciasis), preventing blindness in 11 million children and opening up 25 million hectares of fertile land to farming. Efforts by UN agencies in North Africa in 1991 led to the elimination of the dreaded screworm, a parasite that feeds on human and animal flesh. Other programmes have rescued many from Guinea worm and other tropical diseases.

23 HALTING THE SPREAD OF EPIDEMICS

The World Health Organization helped to stop the spread of severe acute respiratory syndrome (SARS) before it could kill tens of thousands. Following the WHO global alert and the emergency travel advisory issued in March 2003, almost all countries with cases were able to either prevent further transmission or keep the number of additional cases very small. WHO has investigated from 200 to 250 disease outbreaks each year. On average, from 5 to 15 of these annual outbreaks require a major international response.

24 PRESSING FOR UNIVERSAL IMMUNIZATION

Immunization has saved over 20 million lives in the last two decades. As a result of the efforts of UNICEF and the World Health Organization, immunization rates for the six major vaccine-preventable diseases — polio, tetanus, measles, whooping cough, diphtheria and tuberculosis — have risen from under 5 per cent in the early 1970s to about 76 per cent today. Deaths from measles declined about 50 per cent from 1999 to 2005. Immunization against tetanus saved hundreds of thousands of mothers and newborns, and 104 developing countries have eliminated the disease altogether.

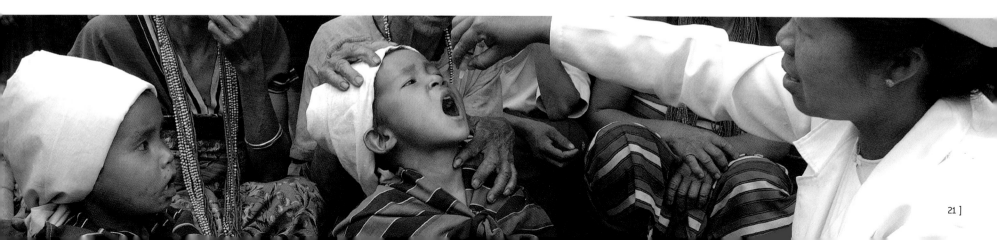

25 REDUCING CHILD MORTALITY

At the start of the 1960s, nearly one in five children died before they were five years old. Through oral rehydration therapy, water and sanitation and other health and nutrition measures undertaken by UN agencies, child mortality rates in the developing countries had dropped to less than one in 12 by 2002. The goal is now to reduce the 1990 under-five mortality rate by two thirds by 2015.

26 LAYING THE GROUNDWORK FOR BUSINESS

The UN is good for business. It has provided the "soft infrastructure" for the global economy by negotiating universally accepted technical standards in such diverse areas as statistics, trade law, customs procedures, intellectual property, aviation, shipping and telecommunications, facilitating economic activity and reducing transaction costs. It has laid the groundwork for investment in developing economies by promoting political stability and good governance, battling corruption and urging sound economic policies and business-friendly legislation.

27 SUPPORTING INDUSTRY IN DEVELOPING COUNTRIES

The United Nations, through the efforts of the UN Industrial Development Organization (UNIDO), has served as a "matchmaker" for North-South and South-South industrial cooperation, promoting entrepreneurship, investment, technology transfer and cost-effective and sustainable industrial development. It has helped countries to manage the process of globalization smoothly and reduce poverty systematically.

28 HELPING DISASTER VICTIMS

When natural disasters and complex emergencies arise, the UN coordinates and mobilizes assistance to the victims. Working together with the Red Cross/Red Crescent and the major aid organizations and donors, the UN operational agencies provide much-needed humanitarian assistance. UN appeals raise more than $2 billion a year for emergency assistance.

29 REDUCING THE EFFECTS OF NATURAL DISASTERS

The World Meteorological Organization (WMO) has helped to spare millions of people from the calamitous effects of both natural and man-made disasters. Its early warning system, which includes thousands of surface monitors, as well as satellites, has made it possible to predict with greater accuracy weather-related disasters, has provided information on the dispersal of oil spills and chemical and nuclear leaks, and has predicted long-term droughts. It has also allowed for the efficient distribution of food aid to drought-affected regions.

30 PROVIDING TSUNAMI RELIEF

Within 24 hours of the tsunami that struck the Indian Ocean on 26 December 2004, UN disaster assessment and coordination teams had been dispatched to the hardest-hit areas. The UN jumped into action to assist the survivors, distributing food to more than 1.7 million individuals, providing shelter for more than 1.1 million made homeless, providing drinking water to more than 1 million and vaccinating more than 1.2 million children against measles, all in the first six months of relief operations. The quick and effective delivery of humanitarian relief meant that no additional lives were lost after the initial day of devastation, and the outbreak of disease was averted.

A TSUNAMI SURVIVOR FINDS A FAMILY PHOTO AMONG THE WRECKAGE.

31 PROTECTING THE OZONE LAYER

The UN Environment Programme (UNEP) and the World Meteorological Organization (WMO) have been instrumental in highlighting the damage caused to Earth's ozone layer. As a result of a treaty known as the Montreal Protocol, the world's Governments are phasing out chemicals that have caused the depletion of the ozone layer, replacing them with safer alternatives. The effort will spare millions of people from the increased risk of contracting skin cancer due to additional exposure to ultraviolet radiation.

32 ADDRESSING CLIMATE CHANGE

The Global Environment Facility (GEF) funds projects to help developing countries reduce the risks of climate change. Established in 1991, GEF is the largest single source of funding for the global environment. It also supports projects to conserve biodiversity, protect the ozone layer, clean up international waters, combat land degradation and phase out toxic organic pollutants. Since 1991, GEF has provided $5.7 billion in grants — including more than 6,000 small grants to non-governmental organizations and community groups — and generated $18.8 billion in co-financing from other partners. The UN Development Programme, the UN Environment Programme and the World Bank are GEF's implementing agencies.

33 CLEARING LANDMINES

The United Nations is leading an international effort to clear landmines in some 30 countries — including Afghanistan, Angola, Bosnia and Herzegovina, Iraq, Mozambique and the Sudan — that still kill and maim thousands of innocent people every year. The UN also works to protect people from danger, help victims to become self-sufficient and assist countries to destroy stockpiled landmines.

34 PROVIDING FOOD TO THE NEEDIEST

The World Food Programme, the world's largest humanitarian agency, reaches on average 90 million hungry people in 80 countries every year, including most of the world's refugees and internally displaced people. WFP food aid is designed to meet the special needs of women and children, those most often affected by hunger. School feeding projects provide free lunches or take-away meals to more than 17 million schoolchildren — with each meal costing just 19 U.S. cents. The agency's logistical capacity spans the technological spectrum, from loading food onto donkeys and yaks to airlifts to satellite networks to monitor deliveries. Over the past four decades, WFP has provided 78.3 million metric tons of food aid to nearly 1.4 billion people in most of the world's poorest countries, an investment of $33.5 billion.

35 FIGHTING HUNGER

The Food and Agriculture Organization of the UN (FAO) leads long-term global efforts to defeat hunger. Serving both developed and developing countries, FAO acts as a neutral forum, where all nations meet as equals to negotiate agreements and debate policy. FAO also helps developing countries to modernize and improve agriculture, forestry and fisheries practices and ensure good nutrition for all.

36 PREVENTING OVERFISHING

Sixteen per cent of the world's fish stocks are overexploited, and 8 per cent have become significantly depleted or are recovering from depletion. FAO monitors marine fishery production and issues alerts to prevent damage caused by overfishing. To address that problem, FAO and its member States have worked together to produce the Code of Conduct for Responsible Fisheries, adopted in 1995.

37 BANNING TOXIC CHEMICALS

The Stockholm Convention on Persistent Organic Pollutants seeks to rid the world of some of the most dangerous chemicals ever created. Adopted in 2001, the UN Convention targets 12 hazardous pesticides and industrial chemicals that can kill people, damage the nervous and immune systems, cause cancer and reproductive disorders and interfere with child development. Other UN conventions and action plans help to protect biodiversity, address climate change, protect endangered species, combat desertification, clean up regional seas and curb cross-border movements of hazardous wastes.

38 PROTECTING CONSUMERS' HEALTH

To ensure the safety of food sold in the marketplace, the Food and Agriculture Organization of the UN and the World Health Organization, working with Member States, have established standards for over 200 food commodities, safety limits for more than 3,000 food containers, and regulations on food processing, transport and storage. Standards on labelling and description work to ensure that the consumer is not misled.

39 COMBATING TERRORISM

The UN has put in place the legal framework to combat international terrorism. Thirteen global legal instruments have been negotiated under UN auspices, including treaties against hostage-taking, aircraft hijacking, terrorist bombings, terrorism financing and, most recently, nuclear terrorism; 63 countries had ratified all of them by June 2005. A new comprehensive convention against terrorism is being drafted. The UN Counter-Terrorism Committee oversees how countries abide by the commitments undertaken in the aftermath of the 11 September terrorist attacks and coordinates counter-terrorism cooperation. The UN Office on Drugs and Crime and other UN agencies have assisted more than 100 countries in strengthening their ability to fight terrorism.

40 PROMOTING REPRODUCTIVE AND MATERNAL HEALTH

The UN Population Fund (UNFPA), by promoting the right of individuals to make their own decisions on how many children to have and when, through voluntary family planning programmes, has helped people to make informed choices and given families, especially women, greater control over their lives. As a result, women in developing countries are having fewer children — from six in the 1960s to three today — slowing world population growth. When UNFPA started work in 1969, under 20 per cent of couples practiced family planning; the number now stands at about 61 per cent. UNFPA and several partners also help to provide skilled attendance at birth, access to emergency obstetrical care and expanded family planning programmes to reduce maternal deaths.

41 HANDING DOWN JUDICIAL SETTLEMENTS IN MAJOR INTERNATIONAL DISPUTES

By giving judgments and advisory opinions, the International Court of Justice has helped settle international disputes involving territorial issues, diplomatic relations, hostage-taking, the right of asylum and economic rights, among others.

42 IMPROVING GLOBAL TRADE RELATIONS

The UN Conference on Trade and Development (UNCTAD) has helped developing countries to negotiate trade agreements and to win preferential treatment for their exports. It has negotiated international commodity agreements to ensure fair prices for developing countries, improved the efficiency of their trade infrastructure and helped them in other ways to diversify their production and to integrate into the global economy.

43 PROMOTING ECONOMIC REFORM

The World Bank and the International Monetary Fund have helped many countries improve their economic management, provided temporary financial assistance to countries to help ease balance-of-payment difficulties and offered training for government finance officials.

44 PROMOTING STABILITY AND ORDER IN THE WORLD'S OCEANS

The UN has spearheaded an international effort to regulate the use of the oceans under a single convention. The 1982 UN Convention on the Law of the Sea, which has gained nearly universal acceptance, provides for the first time a universal legal framework for all activities on and under the oceans. The Convention lays down rules for the establishment of maritime zones, the determination of national maritime jurisdiction, navigation on the high seas, the rights and duties of coastal and other States, the obligation to protect and preserve the marine environment, cooperation in the conduct of marine scientific research, and conservation and sustainable use of marine living resources.

45 IMPROVING AIR AND SEA TRAVEL

UN agencies have been responsible for setting safety standards for sea and air travel. The International Civil Aviation Organization (ICAO) has contributed to making air travel the safest mode of transportation. In 1947, when 9 million travelled by air, 590 were killed in aircraft accidents; in 2004 the number of deaths was 420 out of the 3.3 billion airline passengers. Likewise, the International Maritime Organization (IMO) has helped to make the seas more secure. Statistics show that shipping is becoming safer and is improving its environmental credentials. Ship losses are falling, fatalities are decreasing, pollution incidents are down, total oil pollution is down, and air pollution and pollution from sewage are being tackled — all while the amount of cargo carried by sea continues to increase.

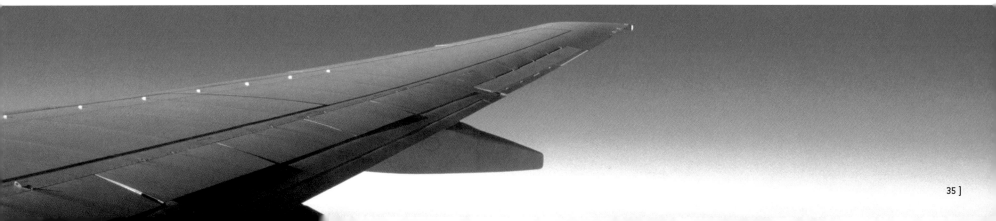

46 TACKLING ILLICIT DRUGS

The UN Office on Drugs and Crime has worked to reduce the supply of, and demand for, illicit drugs, on the basis of the three UN conventions on drug control, as well as to address the social and health consequences of drug abuse, including the drug-related spread of HIV/AIDS. It works by assisting law enforcement agencies, and supporting community-based drug prevention and treatment programmes, as well as initiatives that have helped poor farmers to reduce their reliance on illicit crops by assisting them to shift towards legal and sustainable livelihoods.

47 COMBATING INTERNATIONAL CRIME

The UN Office on Drugs and Crime works with countries and other organizations to counter transnational organized crime with legal and technical assistance to fight corruption, money laundering, drug trafficking, trafficking in persons and smuggling of migrants, as well as by strengthening criminal justice systems. It has played a key role in helping to develop and put into practice relevant international treaties.

48 PROMOTING DECENT WORK

The International Labour Organization (ILO) has put into practice standards and fundamental principles and rights at work, including freedom of association and the right to collective bargaining, the elimination of all forms of forced labour, the abolition of child labour and the elimination of workplace discrimination. Employment promotion, social protection for all and strong social dialogue between employers' and workers' organizations and Governments are at the core of ILO activities.

49 IMPROVING LITERACY AND EDUCATION IN DEVELOPING COUNTRIES

Seventy-six per cent of adults in developing countries can now read and write and 84 per cent of children attend primary school. The goal is now to ensure that all children complete a full course of primary school by 2015. Programmes aimed at promoting education and advancement for women helped to raise the female literacy rate in developing countries from 36 per cent in 1970 to 70 per cent in 2000. The goal is now to ensure that all girls complete primary and secondary school by 2015.

50 GENERATING WORLDWIDE COMMITMENT IN SUPPORT OF CHILDREN

From El Salvador to Lebanon and from the Sudan to the former Yugoslavia, UNICEF has pioneered the establishment of "days of tranquillity" and the opening of "corridors of peace" to provide vaccines and other aid desperately needed by children caught in armed conflict. The Convention on the Rights of the Child has become law in 192 countries. Following the 2002 UN special session on children, 190 Governments committed themselves to a time-bound set of goals in the areas of health, education, protection against abuse, exploitation and violence and the struggle against HIV/AIDS.

51 PRESERVING HISTORIC, CULTURAL, ARCHITECTURAL AND NATURAL SITES

UNESCO has helped 137 countries to protect ancient monuments and historic, cultural and natural sites and has negotiated international conventions to preserve cultural property and outstanding natural sites.

52 FACILITATING ACADEMIC AND CULTURAL EXCHANGES

The United Nations, through UNESCO and the United Nations University, has encouraged scholarly and scientific cooperation, networking of institutions and promotion of cultural expression, including those of minorities and indigenous people.

53 PROTECTING INTELLECTUAL PROPERTY

The World Intellectual Property Organization (WIPO) protects the rights of creators and owners of intellectual property worldwide and ensures that inventors and authors are recognized and rewarded for their ingenuity. Protection of intellectual rights acts as a spur to human creativity, pushing forward the boundaries of science and technology and enriching the world of literature and the arts. By providing a stable environment for the marketing of intellectual property products, it also oils the wheels of international trade.

54 PROMOTING PRESS FREEDOM AND FREEDOM OF EXPRESSION

To allow all people to obtain information that is free of censorship and culturally diverse, UNESCO has helped to develop and strengthen the media and supported independent newspapers and broadcasters. UNESCO also serves as a watchdog for press freedom, publicly denouncing serious violations like the assassination and detention of journalists.

55 TURNING SLUMS INTO DECENT HUMAN SETTLEMENTS

Cities are now home to half of humankind. They are the hub for much national production and consumption — economic and social processes that generate wealth and opportunity. But they also are places of disease, crime, pollution and poverty. In many cities, especially in developing countries, slum-dwellers number more than 50 per cent of the population and have little or no access to shelter, water and sanitation. UN-HABITAT, with over 150 technical programmes and projects in 61 countries around the world, works with Governments, local authorities and non-governmental organizations for innovative solutions for towns and cities. These include providing security of tenure for the urban poor, in turn used as a catalyst for investment in pro-poor housing and basic services.

56 IMPROVING GLOBAL POSTAL SERVICES

The Universal Postal Union (UPU), the primary forum for cooperation among the world's postal services, helps to ensure a truly universal network of up-to-date products and services. It sets the rules for international mail exchanges and makes recommendations to stimulate growth in mail volume and to improve the quality of service for customers. The postal services of UPU's 190 member countries form the largest physical distribution network in the world, processing some 430 billion mail items each year.

57 INTRODUCING IMPROVED AGRICULTURAL TECHNIQUES AND REDUCING COSTS

With assistance from the Food and Agriculture Organization of the UN that has led to improved crop yields, policy reform and local participation, Asian rice farmers have directly saved over $50 million a year on pesticide costs, while their Governments benefited by over $150 million a year through reduced pesticide subsidies. The environmental and health benefits of these pesticide reductions have been estimated at over $10 million per year.

58 PROMOTING THE RIGHTS OF PERSONS WITH DISABILITIES

The United Nations has been at the forefront of the fight for full equality for persons with disabilities, promoting their participation in social, economic and political life. The UN has shown that persons with disabilities are a resource for society, and is drafting the first-ever convention to advance their rights and dignity worldwide.

59 IMPROVING GLOBAL TELECOMMUNICATIONS

The International Telecommunication Union (ITU) brings together Governments and industry to develop and coordinate the operation of global telecommunication networks and services. It has coordinated shared use of the radio spectrum, promoted international cooperation in assigning satellite orbits, worked to improve telecommunication infrastructure in the developing world and negotiated the worldwide standards that assure the seamless interconnection of a vast range of communications systems. From broadband Internet to latest-generation wireless technologies, from aeronautical and maritime navigation to radio astronomy and satellite-based meteorology, from phone and fax services to TV broadcasting and next-generation networks, ITU continues to help the world communicate. Its work has enabled telecommunications to grow into a $1 trillion global industry.

60 IMPROVING THE PLIGHT OF INDIGENOUS PEOPLE

The United Nations has brought to the fore injustices against the 370 million indigenous people who live in 70 countries worldwide and who are among the most disadvantaged and vulnerable groups of people in the world. The 16-member Permanent Forum on Indigenous Issues, established in 2000, works to improve the situation of indigenous people all over the world in development, culture, human rights, the environment, education and health.